mouthmarl

Communion

literary pointillism on a funked-out canvas

Communion

mouthmark series (No. 3)

Published by the mouthmark series, 2006
the pamphlet series of flipped eye publishing
All Rights Reserved

First Edition
Copyright © Jacob Sam-La Rose 2006

Cover Design by Inua Ellams
Series Design © flipped eye publishing, 2006

ISBN-10: 1-905233-05-1
ISBN-13: 978-1-905233-05-2

Supported by
The National Lottery®
through Arts Council England

ARTS COUNCIL
ENGLAND

Communion

Jacob Sam-La Rose

mouthmark *poetry is a kind of literary pointillism applied on a jazz-blues-blood-sex-rock-and-rolled canvas with sweat, tears and spittle as primary colours; if you don't get it you're not listening...*

Contents

Why?

The sound of a letter.
The greatest question, reducing sense
to its smallest indivisible fraction.

A battering ram.

The finest indefatigable blade.
A skeleton key. A house breaker.
Sometimes an ending in itself.

Everything you want it to be.

A Crowd of Sounds

My Mother's Guitar

*"Between my finger and my thumb
The squat pen rests; snug as gun."*
- Digging, Seamus Heaney

Hefting its weight for the first time in years,
wiping the dust from its curves, I want to know
if her mother ever sang to her
the way she sang to me. I was made

for those evenings, cross-legged at her feet,
listening close to each song, strings
chirping against her fingers,
its wide hips notched on her thigh.

Some nights she'd perch on the edge
of her bed, hands crabbed around its neck
and together they'd sing, pulling
thick-throated notes from thin air,

more magic than television. Did her mother
place those melodies under her tongue,
keepsakes to pass down, proof against
the fear of being forgotten? She stopped;

I don't remember when or why,
and I wish I'd learned to play, to hold
the chords she held, catch something of her
voice. The keys turn easily,

tightening the strings back into life
but my fingers don't know how to make
her music. Instead, I write it all down.

Bacchanal

Carnival nights, it was all too easy
      to be caught by the current: a river
         of bodies that flooded the streets,
      anchored to the sounds of floats

loaded with man-sized black boxes,
      monuments to sound, speakers
         whose hearts crackled and snapped,
      near broken with the weight of their own bass.

If you could work through the crush, press
      your hands against a grille, the music would
         breathe on you, itch the air around your fingers
      ring your chest like a gong.

I'd watch from the side, eager
      but too shy to learn the language
         they spoke: the hips and thighs.
      They had their own rolling rhythms,

fluid, fierce and independent.
      The boys I walked with called themselves
         the man dem; had their own brand
      of manners, would almost never ask.

At best, they'd dive headlong
        into that tide, surface and press
                the whisper of a quick hot smile
      up close behind an ear,

behind slicked down curls or pressed hair
        pulled tight to escape the heat.
                Quick hands, snaking around waists,
        pulling themselves forward,

searching for a rhythm to hold
        steady as rock.

Sound

Bright toothed smiles, firefly cigarette butts
and the low, rude lick of a bass line.

Teenage, me and the rest of the boys,
moving through the thick air

of a darkened room, each of us, peeling off
on our own in search of a sticky heat,

drawn by the kinds of moments that bind
couples in dark corners for the length

and breadth of a song. There's one.
One woman, standing alone,

somehow separate from the crush.
Her feet anchored, waistline rolling

as if caught in the swell of some high tide,
the heel of an upturned palm at her temple.

I can imagine a dark wet shadow
pooling in the small of her back

where I'd place my hand having asked her
to dance and learn to match her rhythm,

a rhythm that, even now, across the room
dares me to approach, and yet,

watching, I think I understand
this music, this deep-rooted sound,

how its palpable tremor becomes
her perfect partner.

After Lazerdrome: McDonalds, Peckham Rye...

"What's clear, now, is / that there was music, that it's lasted, that it / doesn't matter whether a player played it, / or whether it just played itself, that it still is / playing, / that at least two gods exist..."
- from 'A Dispute About God', Abdulah Sidran

where I say goodbye to south-east London for the next 3 years
a gaggle of us   still damp   spilling in from the night before

early flock for a Sunday   six or seven a.m.   sleepless
drowning in light and all this quiet   after all that sweat
and darkness   all that flighty noise

this is the year one of the guys says music is the one thing
that won't ever let him down   that music is his religion

the year we're stopped and searched because we
fit the description   the year jungle music passes
out of fashion   stripped down

to naked beat and bass   and we club together   to dance
alone   in the dark   let the music play us   meat and bone

let music fill the empty spaces   rhythm in wads and scads
scattershot   crashing   wall to wall   to be baptised
by filtered drums   pressed snares and swollen b-lines

be baptised by city songs   urban hymns   seamless
sound   a brimming sea of sound   poured out

from towering speaker stacks   this is the year we stand
close enough   to feel the music   rise   its wing-beats
on our faces   drawing salt from our skin   released

then morning   small fries and a strawberry milkshake
counting coins for the cab back   sitting around a table

slouching in moulded seats   drowning in silence
light-headed   leavened   waiting
for the right moment to move

awake for too long   ears
still ringing   drum-drunk

eyes still adjusting to the light
a weight coming down

The Faithful

In my family, church on a Sunday morning was never a matter of choice. I didn't know any arguments that might rescue me from the stiff routine of a starched shirt and neatly seamed strides. Didn't know any prayers. Knew better than to try.

The reverend towered in the pulpit, a flushed neck throttled by the contrast of a pure white collar. He spat sermon into the vaults of echoing empty air above the heads of the congregation. I figured he was selling after-life insurance for the price of a Sunday morning subscription, a sip of *the blood, which was given,* and wafer of bleached, celestial flesh.

Take, eat, this is the body...

It seemed enough to sit there. Daydream. Think of the Sunday morning re-runs of Saturday morning cartoons I was missing. Wonder if it was true that God could see through thoughts like the x-ray specs advertised in the back of every comic book; if it was true that God knew what everyone was thinking, even the thoughts of those few people sleeping in the pews, eyes closed as if marking the passing parables deep in prayer, heads nodding off-beat, almost as if they could hear every word...

On a good day, the sun would stream in through the stained glass, catch the metal of the watch on my wrist and dance a wild, flickering shine across the high, arched ceiling. A shine that, sometimes, became a spotlight, subtle as the gaze of God may possibly have been, if God was ever there, searching for the faces of the faithful.

He never taught me how to hold
a pair of clippers. I never saw him
dab cologne on his cheeks. I don't know
the smell of his sweat, or if our fingers
look alike. I didn't learn to drink
by draining whatever wine he might have left
or sharing an ice cold can. He never
wrestled me down, so I never grew up
to return the favour. I didn't learn to love
music thumbing through his vinyl LPs.
I never woke him. He never once raised
his voice at me. I never heard him laugh,
and although I remember him at the end
of a long distance call, once,
I don't remember his voice,
or what it might have sounded like
saying my name.

Communion

"Make the music with your mouth, Biz!"
- Biz Markie

Street corner spotlights, cupped hands,
spit-crossed palms: solid air pressed
through teeth and lips into high-hats,
kicks, snares and even bass; the moment
passed round like a chalice or smoke,
and riding it all, always, someone
with a need to be heard.

The Spalding Suite

i. Gravity

When we were young, we worshipped stars.

Our symbols of faith were ticks and stripes
endorsed by gleaming long-limbed gods
frozen/framed in the act of impossible flight,
plastered on our walls. For a time we tried
to follow, find the staircase, learn the trick,
to rise, to carve out our own piece of sky
with a butter-smooth arc of an arm
and a Spalding ball glued to the fingertips.
We thought we knew. Sooner or later,
for each of us, gravity came calling
to shackle our ankles and dreams.

But, for a time, we were free.

ii. Again

For a summer, there was only one dream.
We flapped around a court in Shooters Hill,
flanked by tower blocks and the slim figures
of lamp-posts until the light turned soft and bad,
vests cooling where the sweat bled through.
A currency of muscle and finger tips, each of us

hustling hard to earn the calves and inches
needed to break past hand-checks and other
outstretched palms; learning to cover a baseline,
to dance and shuck, make and break
a rhythm of ball and bounce,

hit a bone-hard screen and stay
upright, to palm a ball, still singing
from it's last bounce, and hoist it
like a prayer, all the way to the rim –

an open mouth, responding to everything
with the same silent answer.
Again, it said.

Do it
again.

A rectangle of tarmac. Your slender fingers
and ripening biceps find purpose.

Your wings unfurl, shake loose.

You're learning to time your steps, find
an angle of ascent that allows you to

pause the reel,

hold a heartbeat, draw it out
like a heartfelt sigh.

All you want

is for someone to give you
the gift of your name on the back of

an awed breath,

but the tarmac is teeming with others,
each with his own brand of magic.

The ground

is littered with feathers.
You jostle for air.

iv. Beauty

New Cross. We found a court on a backstreet, hungry
for new ground, eager to test our game against
no one we really knew. Not that any of us

was ever that good. Under a pestle of mid-day sun,
one kid cut through us with a crossover fade, smooth
as any girl's pressed hair. Two steps, up and away,

kissing the ball with his fingers, feeding it through
the hoop. Few things I remember as beautiful.
We stopped, hands on hips, faces twisted

from the effort of trying to keep up, to stop him
from rising. The distance brayed. He belonged
to the air, something we were trying to be,

brought it close enough to touch, and passed us, again
and again. We praised him with a chorus of ragged breath.
Him, already pulling the ball back for the next play.

v. The Brothers of Ladywell Fields

To me, they look like angels, brazen
as broad daylight. I used to run with them,

and I'll tell you the truth: girls never gathered
to watch us swagger or swoop to the rim.

We played for the love of rising
above each other, inhabiting

all that empty air, connecting each step
into nothing with a sure and hard return.

Now, my heartbeat confesses –
I'm vulnerable. My feet stutter

on the tarmac. Maybe the brothers
can read my steps, smell a fall

rising from my skin like sweat.
I know too well the raucous clang

of a near miss on the rim, the way
a smooth arc can turn ugly at the end,

and all that air still remains.
Perhaps I was closer to god.

I haven't held the ball like that
for years.

Clockwork

Brittle

I was always a serious child.
I never believed

that a lost tooth, buried
under a pillow and a wish

could be resurrected
as some dream come true.

I knew it would be there,
each morning, still

the same small nugget
of dirty pearl,

crusted in blood,
evermore brittle.

The Hours

My other father - the one that stayed - worked nights when I was a kid. I've never understood nightshifts, although I've pulled them since, making my business while everything else rests; never understood the way the sun comes up like laughter over your shoulder, some private joke. Lonely hours, home to all the essential undesirable occupations that keep the world ticking over, push it through into another day. He drove a mail truck up and down the country and always came back at four or five in the morning - hours I was only dimly aware of, hours my body passed through in sleep, like ghost towns between cities. At first, I slept light, woken by the sound of his key in the lock, a foreign thing. Soon, I learned to sleep through. Some nights I woke when his feet took the stairs, slow, with care, so as to keep the hour sacred, undisturbed.

Algebra
For OPRF High School, Chicago

I'm 29 in a high school maths lesson.
I've had dreams like this. Nightmares.

The teacher speaks a different language,
a vocabulary of numbers. Inconsistent graphs.
Tests. Slopes. $x+y$. $y=3x-2$. I daydream that

maybe there's music in these numbers.
If x were a tree and y were a sound,
negative a over b might =

the Chicagoan wind, a fiddlestick of air
making leaves sing. I imagine black notes
rolling down a woman's cheek.

Last night, I saw a woman cry,
stunned by the strength of her own words
scored on a page, a flood of memory.

There are numbers everywhere.
The teacher gives two methods of solving
equations: substitution or elimination.

The woman that cried has three siblings.
She, the only one that kept her mother's Xmas bow.
She hasn't seen her mother for seven months.

Immigration = a blank wall with no doors,
dividing her family, crowned by an eagle
looking down from a nest of barbed wire.

The teacher points to the board and asks
is this consistent? A student asks if this is the point
of intersection. The woman that shed tears

doesn't know if she'll see her mother again,
and there's a music in everything: in chalk
tapping out problems and solutions on a board,

in layers of chalk dust falling on a classroom floor
like passing minutes, in school bells marking
a lesson's end, in tears coaxed into words.

And where there's music, there's beauty.

Pendulum

The girl on front desk in reception will probably keep the baby.
The boy in the office behind her doesn't know what to do.
One night, after hours, you sit on a cold brick wall,
your arm around her shoulders, holding her together
as the tears come too suddenly for her to speak
and she cries into her palms, too weak to stand.
You want to help. He's not there. She calls it love.

It's beginning to rain as it often does in movies
at moments like this, and you don't know it yet,
but there will be phone calls. She will drag you out of sleep,
her voice blurred with questions. Hours will pass.
Some nights, the way she describes him will chime
with the shadows chased across your wall by passing headlights.
Days from now, she will show you his picture in her wallet, back
behind the plastic with other important things, smiling
as if he never left. It will dizzy you.

You will learn to guarantee that nothing stays the same,
that everything moves. You will remember a physics lesson,
a teacher that spoke of constant flux. A pendulum's swinging weight.
But you won't be able to find any way to stop that pendulum's
back and forth, any more than you could stop
one minute bleeding into the next.
The best you can do, now, is hold her close,
and strain to hear, somewhere deep inside her,
a different clock beginning to mark it's own time.

Clockwork

Shadows come to power - night
settles in. An absence of light
defied by streetlamps and signage.

The window is closed, every sound
silenced by the soft-edged stench
of bleach, mopped floors and sterile sheets.

Then, in her sleep, she turns. He unlocks
his fingers from hers. Moves to pull
the curtains. He wants to press his face

against the glass, feel a cold shock
blaze across his cheek, watch his breath
mist and spread, some important part of him,

visible in front of the world. Outside,
there's still the clockwork of taillights,
and above, travelling inexorably,

the hulking forms of clouds,
the blind weight of all that air.

Autumn

i.

...and the sun's light is a bleached smear on a soiled rag. Anything ever pinned to the sky must finally kiss the ground. Leaves, bruised by brighter days, fall like plucked feathers. Trees flame until they bare themselves against an ashen sky; spent, bleeding into the colours of used pennies, they'll never burn this way again.

ii.

She left. Plain and simple. He imagines himself a room, void of furniture, empty and cavernous, light bleeding in through flat grey slats. No heat in the air; water waiting silent and solid in the pipes. Her laughter echoes from the walls. The sound of her voice settles like dust on the hardwood floor.

Seconds

Anything past the horizon / is invisible, it can only be imagined. You
want to see the future but / you only see the sky.
- Road Music, Richard Siken

Late night, flicking through stations on the car stereo
you tune in on a rasping voice, hoisted
over lilting acoustic chords; a song
you've never heard before. The road opens
in front of you, and there's nothing about this song
you don't already know, even down to the rasp,

the way the voice is honeyed with heartache,
the rough edge calculated to sound raw
and real. Every note is second hand.
And maybe there's some other place you need to be.
Somewhere else, where something is happening,
without you, now, something so vital

that it calls out from wherever it is,
and you don't know how to get there.
Maybe you're not driving. Maybe you're trying
to put words down on a blindingly blank page.
Maybe you're trying to get dressed.
Or maybe your hands are resting lightly

on the back of the neck of the person
you're supposed to love now,
and maybe, for a moment,
you can't tell the difference
between that neck
and any other neck you've known.

Aubade

Waking, you find yourself on a balcony, hands clasped over the edge, forearms resting too hard on the cool black railing. A room falling back into shadow through the open door behind you. You never thought it would be so easy to push back the arm that lay across you, skin sticking to the skin. To rise without a pause to wonder whether the empty impression you'd leave would be noticed, the shadow on the mattress, testament to where you'd spent the night.

Waking, you run your tongue over your teeth. Lick the salt from your lips. Spit. Crane forward to see it fall. Your eyes unsure of what to do with all the silence. Every other window in the opposite block curtained and closed. No movement in the sunrise. No distant hush of traffic. No song. Nothing, except the dark shape of a body stood by a stoplight on the corner below. The dark shape of a man, his face turned up towards you, so still he could be chiselled stone, sculpted. So still that he belongs to this morning, to the cars parked and driverless and the shadows clinging to the ground beneath them.

You perch there, hands clasped over the edge, looking down at him. Realising he may not see you. Maybe he, too, is looking for something in the pinks and blues of this half-lit morning sky. Maybe he, like you, wonders how long this moment can last. Maybe there's a woman in a room behind him that will wake soon, reach out and feel him gone. And regardless of whether he sees you or not, you raise a hand to your head in mock salute. Knowing that he, like you, is simply waiting. Waiting to see how long it will be before something, again, begins to move. Waiting to see what happens next.

Freedom

To write this, I remember a night too hot
to sleep – a night on which the single window
refused to shift, and the room sweltered.

That night, I dragged myself downstairs,
jealous of the child my cousin used to be,

his talent for hard sleep. In sleep, his body
danced, loose, unguarded, trying to find
a shape it felt it fit, willing to walk the corridor

to the front room, where you'd find him
next morning, face down on the couch, slender

fingers trailing on the floor, him oblivious
and innocent, asking who'd moved him in the night.
Now he's grown. Grown into a world

in which even sleep is scrutinised, a bed that's not
his own, a hankering for home-cooked food.

He serves a time defined by walls. Wardens.
Wishes. If I could, I'd wish him back.
I'd wish him home, and I'd watch over him again

as he sleeps. The shapes his body takes,
and what they say of freedom.

about Jacob Sam-La Rose

Well known for a brand of intimately detailed and finely crafted poetry, Jacob Sam-La Rose has been described as "the backbone of the London poetry scene". Poet, writer, tutor, artistic director and performer, his programme of international appearances has taken him as far afield as Kiasma - the Museum of Contemporary Art in Helsinki, Chicago State University, Mylos Theatre (Greece), the Center of Contemporary Art in Glasgow, and London's Queen Elizabeth Hall, as well as a range of more conventional poetry and spoken word venues. He also runs the FYI mailing lists (www.metaroar.com), which are essential if you're interested in poetry and spoken word, and directs a range of initiatives for young, developing writers.

http://www.jsamlarose.com

Lightning Source UK Ltd.
Milton Keynes UK
UKHW040707100519

342454UK00001B/431/P